Bee Adventurous with Words

You can do it!
Friends   Travel
Enjoy Family Listen
Smile Love
Hugs
Sunshine Care
Bee Kisses
grateful

Written by
Beverly Bruemmer

Illustrated by
Seth Fitts

Vabella Publishing
P.O. Box 1052
Carrollton, Georgia 30112
www.vabella.com

Manufactured in the United States of America

ISBN 978-1-957479-79-8

Your birth announcement

Your first birthday memory

Your best Christmas memory

Your first memory of school

Your best high school memory

Your first date

Your prom date

Your best friends
through the years

List ten things that make you happy

Your best holiday memory

Write a letter to your favorite teacher

Write about a funny incident

List your last act of
random kindness

Write about an
influential person

Write about the memories an old photo inspires

What advice would you give your past or future self?

List 30 things that make you happy

What would be the title of your life story

Write your obituary